GW00788147

everything you need to know...fast

FUNDRAISING DATABASES
An Introduction to the
Setup and Use

by **Peter Flory**
reviewed by Caroline Hukins

WIREMILL
PUBLISHING LTD

Across the world the organizations and institutions that fundraise to finance their work are referred to in many different ways. They are charities, non-profits or not-for-profit organizations, non-governmental organizations (NGOs), voluntary organizations, academic institutions, agencies, etc. For ease of reading, we have used the term Nonprofit Organization, Organization or NPO as an umbrella term throughout the *Quick*Guide series. We have also used the spellings and punctuation used by the author.

Published by
Wiremill Publishing Ltd.
Edenbridge, Kent TN8 5PS, UK
info@wiremillpublishing.com
www.wiremillpublishing.com
www.quickguidesonline.com

British Library Cataloguing in Publication Data
A catalogue record for this book is available from the British Library.

ISBN Number 1-905053-10-X

Printed by Rhythm Consolidated Berhad, Malaysia
Cover Design by Jennie de Lima and Edward Way
Design by Colin Woodman Design

CONTENTS

FUNDRAISING DATABASES

AN INTRODUCTION TO THE
SETUP AND USE

INTRODUCTION

The fundraising database is likely to be the most important system you will run on your computer network. It will also be the most expensive, the most complex, and the most resource-hungry. There are a huge number from which to choose. You can't afford to select the wrong one.

This guide illustrates the importance of a good database, the considerations relevant to choosing one, and the range of ways it can help your organisation. It also offers practical advice about managing the many functions available.

A second Quick*Guides* volume, "Fundraising Databases – Adapting for Different Needs", provides a more detailed discussion of how the database can be adapted to meet the needs of the specific types of fundraising carried out within your NPO.

Throughout this guide there are illustrations from various database programmes available on the market. These are for demonstration purposes only, and not suggestions of what you should purchase for your organisation.

What Can the Database Do for Your Organisation?

The database is a means of storing information without cumbersome paper records, and has huge advantages of space and accessibility.

- It can store information indefinitely, and delete it automatically after a specified period.

- It can make selections using different criteria.

- It can generate letters and receipts from the data held.

- It can show links between supporters.

- It can display plans and reminders that have been programmed in.

- It can allow you to import and export data as necessary from external organisations such as banks or list brokers.

- It provides the opportunity for reports to be produced from the data held, facilitating analysis and performance measurement.

And these examples only begin to illustrate the range and potential of the database.

Chosen correctly and operated properly, the database can be your best friend. Choose incorrectly and the database can be an ongoing source of irritation and frustration.

How Do You Choose a Database?

Compare prices and information from a selection of potential providers before making this decision, and seek advice from others in the non-profit sector. There is much to consider, and the decision is an important one.

Consider all the functions for which the database will be used. Discuss requirements with everyone who will be involved in using it (or in a larger organisation, nominate a representative of each function).

Consider the following areas as a minimum.

- Initial investigations. What is on the market? What are other people doing?

- Define your objectives. Why do you want a new or different database?

- Define your requirements - so you know what you are looking for.

- Define selection criteria in order to make an informed choice.

- Go out to tender. Use formal procedures so that you don't get taken in.

- Analyse the tenders. Compare like with like.

- See demonstrations. Would you be happy using it?

- Take up references. Are other users happy?

- Make the choice – the big decision.

Meet with your chosen provider several times to satisfy yourself that you have made the right decision. Ensure that more than one person in your organisation is involved, and take notes during meetings. It is a far-reaching decision, and you cannot afford to lose the research findings and rationale if the person responsible should fall sick or leave the organisation.

Reviewer's Comment
It is easy to feel intimidated or unsure when dealing with database providers. They may use terms with which you are unfamiliar. It is crucial that you understand what is being proposed and whether it will work for you. Take your time. Have numerous demonstrations. Consult widely. Ask questions until you understand.

DATA ITEMS

The database must store all the data you need and anticipate what you may need in the future.

As a minimum you must store:

- The names and addresses of your supporters.

- How much they have given you.

- When donations were made.

- The purpose of the donations.

From there you can add a whole host of items such as:

- Mailing indicators (what you can send to them and when).

- Mailing history (what you have actually sent them).

- The interests of supporters.

- Events that supporters have attended.

- Supporters' preferred means of communication.

Consider the different data items needed for different types of supporters. Many or even most data items will be the same for every type of supporter, but some will apply only to individuals, some only to trusts and foundations and other grantmakers, some only to companies, etc. The database must allow for the differences as well as the similarities.

It is important that the database allows you to add new data at a later date. You won't be able to think of everything you need initially, and your fundraising methods are likely to change over time.

Reviewer's Comment
You may be asked to define what information you want the database to store. Look at a number of databases and the way they are set up for inspiration. Don't be afraid to be wrong or to miss something – this has happened to everyone.

Data must be quickly and easily accessible. You will frequently need to search the database to find specific supporter records. The usual searches are made by supporter number (each supporter should have a unique reference number), supporter name, and elements of the address such as town or postal code. Searching by other data items is often useful (for example, telephone number or email address). Sometimes you may be searching while a supporter waits on the telephone, so speed and ease of use are important.

Data must be clear and easy to navigate. Not everything you store about a supporter will fit onto one display screen, so it must be obvious where the data is and how to reach it. Most systems have an initial screen showing basic data such as name and address, with a clearly labelled set of tabs or buttons (e.g., "Donations" or "Events Attended") showing where other data can be found.

Basic supporter data as shown in database The Raiser's Edge

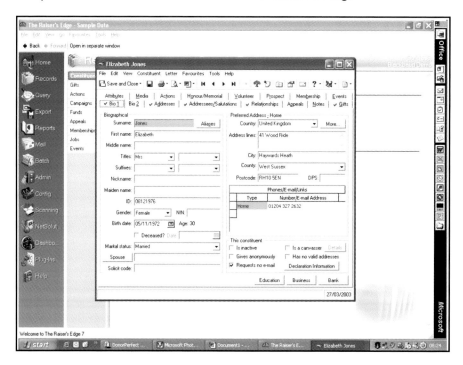

Maintaining Accurate Data

The way data is stored is the bedrock of the database. Get it wrong and your database is almost useless; get it right and your database is the most effective fundraising tool at your disposal.

One of the biggest problems with databases is duplicate records. Your database must be able to search and report on potential duplicate records using a variety of name and address criteria.

Deciding whether two records are actually duplicates is a human process, so when the user has decided that two records are the same person or organisation, then the system must be able to merge these records into one. The user will specify which record is to be kept and the system will then pull all subsidiary data (e.g., donations, event attendances, etc.) across to this record and delete the duplicate record.

The next biggest problem is that of incorrect addresses. Databases must be cleaned regularly. In some countries, special postal-code software exists to help with this task.

Another major problem is incomplete data, such as partial addresses or donations with no campaign code (what prompted the donation) or fund code (what the money will be used for). These need to be listed and reviewed regularly.

An audit trail of who did what to each record and when can be useful in maintaining accurate and consistent data. At the very least, you need to know who created the record and when, and who last amended it and when.

If the database is to remain a useful tool for all users, then it is important to establish universal codes and forms of data entry. For example, dates should be programmed to appear in the same format. All users should be trained to use codes in the same way, and the ability to create new codes should be limited to one or two people.

Security here does not refer to a system backup (that is taken for granted) but to security over the data. Personal information is confidential, and the database may necessarily hold information of a sensitive nature. Typical data restrictions could be:

■ Restricting a user to specific functions or menus. This is useful for volunteers who have specific tasks to perform and do not need to see other parts of the system. This makes the system easier for them to learn and use.

■ Restricting a user to specific types of operations by defining who can view data, who can enter data, and who can alter the data. For example, to maintain the financial integrity of the system, you might restrict the alteration and reversal of donations to the accounting department.

Example of user security restrictions from database Advantage Fundraiser

- Restricting a user to specific sets of contact records. This is useful for ensuring that only people with an interest in certain types of contacts can see those records, thus limiting who can access sensitive data. For example, beneficiary records (which may be linked to donor records) may only need to be accessed by the service provision department.

- Restricting access to specific parts of records. For example, keep celebrity addresses confidential to a selected set of users, but allow other users to see that the celebrities exist on the database.

- Restricting a user to running certain selections, mailings and reports but not others.

Reviewer's Comment
Ensure that the policy for access is clearly stated and applied so people aren't confused or angry when they can't access some part of the database.

Once it holds all the data you need, a database can greatly assist in raising money from people or organisations with something in common. Computers can easily link records together and can remember far more links than any human brain.

For example, it may be useful to view such links as:

Individual to individual – linking one person to another person can show family relationships, who knows whom, and who works with whom.

Individual to organisation – linking people to organisations can reflect such important relationships as employee/employer, trustee/trust, director/company, and chairman/local fundraising group.

Organisation to organisation – linking organisations together can reflect such things as parent company/subsidiary company, company/company trust, and local group/regional group.

Supporter "relationship tree" as shown in database Progress

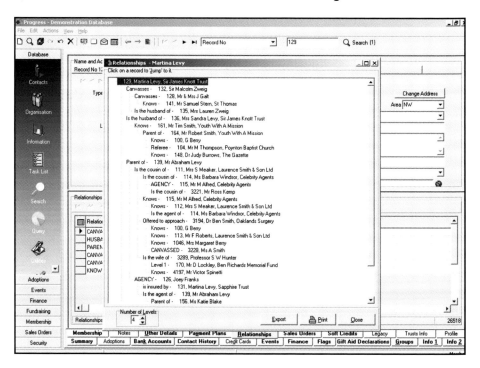

CONTACT RELATIONSHIPS

When developing the necessary functions for the database, consider the following:

Reciprocation – it is important that every relationship between two supporters has a reverse relationship and that one-way links are avoided so that links can be followed down the tree and back up again.

"From" and "to" dates – adding the beginning and end dates to relationships can be useful to show current and past committee membership, past presidents, and employment history.

Tree structures – if all of a supporter's relationships are shown in a "tree" format, then you can follow links from one supporter to another supporter to another supporter and see how they all link up and whether they are individuals or organisations.

Jumping or switching – you must be able to start by looking at the details of one supporter, viewing this supporter's relationships and then "jumping" or "switching" to viewing the details of any other supporter in the tree (and switching back again).

SEGMENTING, SELECTING AND MAILING

Segmentation of a database is the bringing together of contacts with similar characteristics that you wish to approach in the same way (people or organisations that have things in common).

For example, it may be useful to segment based on donation history (how much the donors have given, when they last gave, and how often they have given), on geography (where they live), or on demography (age ranges, social class, income level, religion, marital status, and a host of other lifestyle characteristics).

Once your database is segmented, you can then select one or more segments for a particular fundraising approach. You may wish to send out a mailing by using a word-processing Mail Merge function, either by printing personalised letters or producing personalised labels to attach to pre-prepared mailing packs. You can also print a list of people in a selection set for use in a telephone campaign (assuming that you have recorded their telephone numbers!).

The process of selection requires complex logic such as:

- Being able to include or exclude records with specified data values (specific information).

- Being able to define rules on data items held in any and all the data tables in the database.

- Being able to use all logical operators such as "and," "or," "not."

- Being able to bring all of the above together as "selection criteria" in a single statement.

- Being able to merge selection sets together to form supersets.

- Being able to split selection sets into subsets.

- Being able to define a hierarchy of selection sets so that people who meet the criteria for several selection sets get treated in the most appropriate way and only get one mailing (i.e., their record is ignored when dealing with selections lower in the hierarchy even though they meet the criteria).

Selections can be:

Standard – the same criteria used many times.

Regular – criteria that can be changed at runtime (e.g., dates).

Ad-hoc – different criteria defined every time.

A '1 in N' function is a useful feature in selections. For example, if you can select one record in every 10 records from your selection and mail only this 10 percent of your selection, you can use it as a test; depending upon the results of this "test mailing," you can decide whether to mail the other 90 percent. This can spare the organisation from proceeding with costly campaigns that yield poor results.

A very important addition to the mailing process is the generation of a "mailing history" record that shows exactly who has sent what to whom and when. Similarly, the creation of a telephone contact record should show who contacted whom, when and what was said.

Example search criteria form database Donor 2000

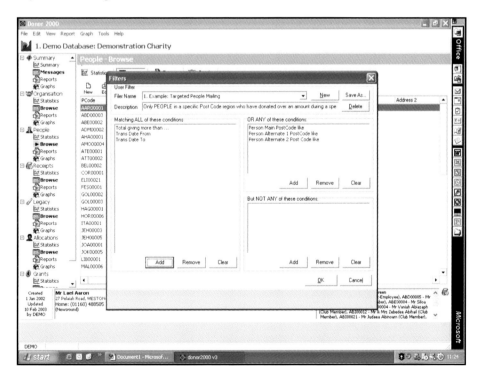

The result of contacting your supporters will be money (we hope!). For audit purposes, and in order to analyse your income and plan future campaigns, you must record this money item by item. You need to know:

■ Who the donation is from.

■ The date of the donation.

■ The amount of the donation.

■ What prompted the donation.

■ What the donation is for.

■ Whether a receipt is required.

If a small number of donations are received per day, they can be entered into the database one at a time by finding the appropriate donor's record and entering the details of the donation.

For a larger number of donations per day (say 50 or more), a greater measure of financial control is required, necessitating the use of "batch processing". A batch is a manageable number of donations (usually 20 to 30) grouped together, with a control document that contains the number of items and the total value of these items. The control information is entered into the system before the individual items and is used to check that no data-entry errors are made.

During the entry of income items, a number of important functions are required:

■ The ability to "split" a single gift into amounts for different purposes (e.g., half for one project and half for another project, or, three quarters for membership and a quarter for general funds).

■ The ability to "soft credit" a gift to another supporter e.g., a gift given by Mrs A in memory of Mr B, or annual membership for Miss C paid for by Mr D. In these examples the real money amounts would be recorded against Mrs A and Mr D but a note would appear on the records of Mr B and Miss C showing that the money had been paid on their behalf.

■ The ability to "hot-key" to other functions during the entry of a batch. You will sometimes need to break off from the entry of an item to search for a supporter record or to change an address, and then return to the batch entry process.

■ The ability to change anything in the batch before it is finalised but NOT to delete or change amounts once the number of items and the total of the items match the batch control.

After the completion of a batch, the following functions are required:

■ **Reversal** – for money never received such as a bounced cheque.

■ **Refund** – for returning money received to a supporter.

■ **Transaction amendment** – to change any element of the income item when an error is discovered at a later date. Controls are required here, especially if the amount is to be changed.

Once the income has been entered, the database should produce a summary (or detail) report of batches for a single day (or other time period) that can be used as a control document when the money is deposited in a bank.

Donation entry from database Progress

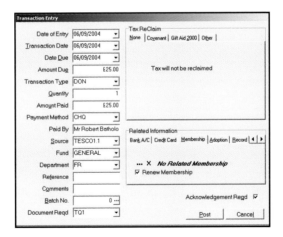

THANK YOU LETTERS

Nearly all supporters expect to be thanked for making a donation. They might also reasonably expect your response to be personal (not a standard letter that says "Dear Supporter") and the data you hold about them to be correct.

The production of thank you letters can be done via a link to a Mail Merge process in a standard word-processing system, with the facility to incorporate the following features:

- A personal salutation.

- The amount of the donation (rather than just saying "Thank you for your kind donation").

- A paragraph relevant to the project on which the money will be spent.

- Amending/personalising letters, both singly and globally, before they are printed.

- Mail Merge to a letter or an email depending on the supporter's preference.

- Production of formal receipts as well as, or instead of, thank you letters, if requested.

Don't produce a letter if the supporter has requested no acknowledgment (either for a single donation or all donations).

Also don't produce a thank you letter for every donation of a regular commitment, but produce one for the first donation and perhaps a special one on every anniversary.

CUSTOMER SERVICE

The database makes it easier to employ high standards of customer care. It has enough flexibility that people's individual preferences can be recorded and easily seen, and prompts may be entered to remind you of what has been said in the past.

It is essential to store and use indicators or flags to ensure that your supporters get what they want from your organisation, when and how they want it. Thus, promotions can be tailored to individual preferences. And because some organisations swap lists with other nonprofit organisations, an indicator that shows whether someone consents to your sharing their name with other organisations is also useful.

It is helpful to be able to print a simple report containing all of the data you hold on the database for a selected supporter so that the supporter can inform you of any errors or omissions.

It is useful to have a direct link from the database to a word-processing system in order to create a single ad-hoc letter to a supporter.

On rare occasions, you will get complaints from supporters. These complaints and the actions taken as a result can be recorded on the database. Problem areas can then be reported on and analysed.

Set up information prior to printing thank you letters from database The Raiser's Edge

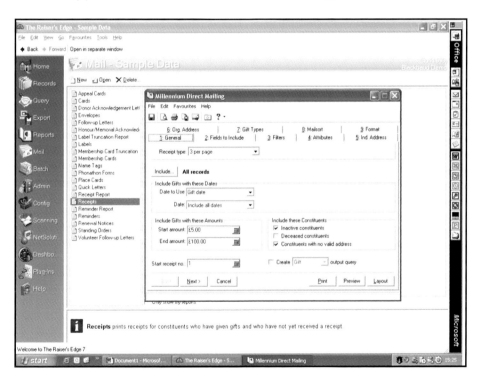

Reporting and Analysis

Once the database stores all of the requisite data, any number of reports and analyses can be produced. A good database will have a predefined set of standard fundraising reports.

Standard reports might include:

- All donations for a batch, for a day, for a week or a month.
- A donation summary for a day, week, month or year to date.
- A donation summary by campaign/appeal.
- A donation summary by fund/project.
- A donation summary by donation type.
- A list of regular payments that were expected but not received.
- A report on current pledges with the status and balance of each one.
- A list of highest donations for the day, week, month, year.
- Soft credit list.

- Sponsorship report.
- Financial reconciliation.
- Audit report.
- Counts of supporters in specified categories.

More sophisticated analysis reports might include:

- Cash flow.
- ROI (return on investment) for campaigns/appeals.
- Pareto analysis (the 80:20 rule applied to fundraising).
- RFV (recency/frequency/value) analysis (sometimes known as RFM (recency/frequency/ monetary value).

Additional functions

Statistical analysis reports like Pareto and RFV should also enable the user to see the actual supporters in each analysis grouping and to select each group for mailing.

It must be possible to output all reports to other systems such as spreadsheets for further analysis, or to word-processing for publication.

The database must allow the user to change standard reports to fit the needs of his or her organisation as required. It must also have a report-writing function to allow the user to create new reports.

There is an increasing trend for database suppliers to make the data structures of their databases accessible so that fundraisers can use commercial report-writing software products to create new reports. A word of warning is required here because producing your own reports can be extremely complex.

Sample standard reports list from database DonorPerfect

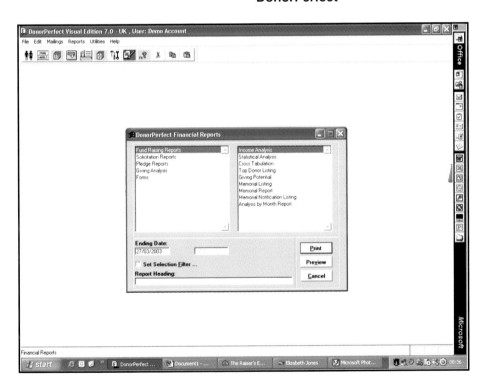

Importing and Exporting Data

It is important to be able to get data into the database quickly and easily, and then be able to get it back out again. Frequently data may need to be imported or exported in bulk, e.g., from the bank, from external agencies, or from companies that manage outsourced fundraising projects, or from list brokers for mail shot contacts.

When importing data, you must be able to:

- Import every external field into your database (initially when taking data from another system).

- Import names and addresses (when buying lists to build up your database).

- Import donation items (if you have large campaigns for which you cannot handle the volume of responses and you outsource the data capture to a third party).

- Import from a variety of file formats and from the Internet.

- Import files on a temporary basis only.

- Check for duplicate records as new records are imported and, when a potential duplicate record is identified, offer the user the option to accept or reject the imported record. The criteria for checking duplicates must be under the control of the user.

- Import records that create new supporter records, or that update data in existing supporter records. The update function can be useful for adding demographic indicators to supporter records; or when some form of manipulation has been carried out on the data within another system; or for "global updating," when you want to set one or more fields to the same values for a specified set of records.

When exporting data, you must be able to:

- Export the entire database in an industry standard format (for security purposes, and also because you might want to change to another database at some time in the future).

IMPORTING AND EXPORTING DATA

- Export names and addresses (for sending data to a mailing house to send out a large mailing).

- Export income items (for external analysis in a spreadsheet or a specialist statistics system).

- Export summary income data (for reporting purposes or for input into an accounting system).

Exporting data to Excel from database Donor2000

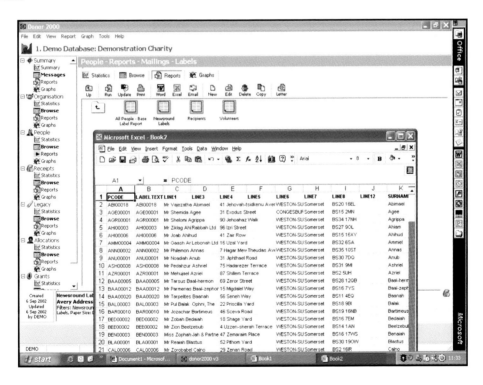

FINAL THOUGHTS

C hoosing the right database, training users to get maximum value from it, and briefing users to use it in a uniform way will take time. However, if managed properly, it can be the most rewarding investment your organisation makes. It can add immeasurably to the efficiency of the organisation's financial processing, to customer service, and to the evaluation of performance.

Look after your database, use it wisely and benefit from it.